ADVENTURE TIME™

MAD LIBS®

concept created by Roger Price & Leonard Stern

PSS!
PRICE STERN SLOAN
An Imprint of Penguin Group (USA) Inc.

PRICE STERN SLOAN
Published by the Penguin Group
Penguin Group (USA) Inc., 375 Hudson Street, New York, New York 10014, USA
Penguin Group (Canada), 90 Eglinton Avenue East, Suite 700,
Toronto, Ontario M4P 2Y3, Canada
(a division of Pearson Penguin Canada Inc.)
Penguin Books Ltd., 80 Strand, London WC2R 0RL, England
Penguin Group Ireland, 25 St. Stephen's Green, Dublin 2, Ireland
(a division of Penguin Books Ltd.)
Penguin Group (Australia), 250 Camberwell Road, Camberwell, Victoria 3124, Australia
(a division of Pearson Australia Group Pty. Ltd.)
Penguin Books India Pvt. Ltd., 11 Community Centre,
Panchsheel Park, New Delhi—110 017, India
Penguin Group (NZ), 67 Apollo Drive, Rosedale, Auckland 0632, New Zealand
(a division of Pearson New Zealand Ltd.)
Penguin Books (South Africa) (Pty.) Ltd., 24 Sturdee Avenue,
Rosebank, Johannesburg 2196, South Africa

Penguin Books Ltd., Registered Offices:
80 Strand, London WC2R 0RL, England

Published by Price Stern Sloan, a division of Penguin Young Readers Group,
345 Hudson Street, New York, New York 10014.

ISBN 978-0-8431-7221-8

1 3 5 7 9 10 8 6 4 2

MAD LIBS®
INSTRUCTIONS

MAD LIBS® is a game for people who don't like games!
It can be played by one, two, three, four, or forty.

• RIDICULOUSLY SIMPLE DIRECTIONS

In this tablet you will find stories containing blank spaces where words
are left out. One player, the READER, selects one of these stories. The
READER does not tell anyone what the story is about. Instead, he/she asks
the other players, the WRITERS, to give him/her words. These words are
used to fill in the blank spaces in the story.

• TO PLAY

The READER asks each WRITER in turn to call out a word—an adjective or
a noun or whatever the space calls for—and uses them to fill in the blank
spaces in the story. The result is a MAD LIBS® game.

When the READER then reads the completed MAD LIBS® game to the other
players, they will discover that they have written a story that is fantastic,
screamingly funny, shocking, silly, crazy, or just plain dumb—depending
upon which words each WRITER called out.

• EXAMPLE (*Before* and *After*)

"_____!" he said _____
      EXCLAMATION   ADVERB

as he jumped into his convertible _____ and
                                        NOUN

drove off with his _____ wife.
                      ADJECTIVE

"*Ouch*!" he said *Stupidly*
      EXCLAMATION   ADVERB

as he jumped into his convertible *cat* and
                                          NOUN

drove off with his *brave* wife.
                      ADJECTIVE

MAD LIBS
QUICK REVIEW

In case you have forgotten what adjectives, adverbs, nouns, and verbs are, here is a quick review:

An ADJECTIVE describes something or somebody. *Lumpy*, *soft*, *ugly*, *messy*, and *short* are adjectives.

An ADVERB tells how something is done. It modifies a verb and usually ends in "ly." *Modestly*, *stupidly*, *greedily*, and *carefully* are adverbs.

A NOUN is the name of a person, place, or thing. *Sidewalk*, *umbrella*, *bridle*, *bathtub*, and *nose* are nouns.

A VERB is an action word. *Run*, *pitch*, *jump*, and *swim* are verbs. Put the verbs in past tense if the directions say PAST TENSE. *Ran*, *pitched*, *jumped*, and *swam* are verbs in the past tense.

When we ask for A PLACE, we mean any sort of place: a country or city (*Spain*, *Cleveland*) or a room (*bathroom*, *kitchen*).

An EXCLAMATION or SILLY WORD is any sort of funny sound, gasp, grunt, or outcry, like *Wow!*, *Ouch!*, *Whomp!*, *Ick!*, and *Gadzooks!*

When we ask for specific words, like a NUMBER, a COLOR, an ANIMAL, or a PART OF THE BODY, we mean a word that is one of those things, like *seven*, *blue*, *horse*, or *head*.

When we ask for a PLURAL, it means more than one. For example, *cat* pluralized is *cats*.

MAD LIBS® is fun to play with friends, but you can also play it by yourself! To begin with, DO NOT look at the story on the page below. Fill in the blanks on this page with the words called for. Then, using the words you have selected, fill in the blank spaces in the story.

Now you've created your own hilarious MAD LIBS® game!

ALL ABOUT JAKE AND FINN

ANIMAL _____

PLURAL NOUN _____

VERB ENDING IN "ING" _____

ADJECTIVE _____

NOUN _____

NOUN _____

NOUN _____

ADJECTIVE _____

ADVERB _____

VERB _____

NOUN _____

ADJECTIVE _____

A PLACE _____

VERB ENDING IN "ING" _____

MAD LIBS®
ALL ABOUT
JAKE AND FINN

Jake the _____ and Finn the Human are not only best
                  ANIMAL

_____, they're also brothers. When Finn was a little baby,
   PLURAL NOUN

Jake's parents found him in the woods _____ by himself.
                                      VERB ENDING IN "ING"

Now the buddies live together in their way-_____ Tree
                                              ADJECTIVE

Fort in the _____ Lands section of Ooo. While they may
               NOUN

be as close as two peas in a/an _____, there are a few
                                     NOUN

differences between them. Jake's got magical stretchy powers and can

make himself as big as a/an _____ or as _____
                                 NOUN   ADJECTIVE

as a worm. While Jake gets _____ sidetracked, Finn wants
                                ADVERB

nothing more than to get up and _____. With a cross-
                                        VERB

_____ and sword by his side, Finn is really _____
   NOUN   ADJECTIVE

at taking down evil. Finn is superbrave and would go to the ends

of (the) _____ to help anyone who is up against bad
           A PLACE

vibes. One thing's for sure—both dudes are always down for some

adventure time and a gut-_____ laugh!
                          VERB ENDING IN "ING"

From ADVENTURE TIME MAD LIBS® • ™ & © Cartoon Network. (s12
Published by Price Stern Sloan, an imprint of Penguin Group (USA) Inc., 345 Hudson Stree

MAD LIBS® is fun to play with friends, but you can
play it by yourself! To begin with, DO NOT look
story on the page below. Fill in the blanks on this
with the words called for. Then, using the words you h
selected, fill in the blank spaces in the story.

Now you've created your own hilarious MAD LIBS® game!

JAKE THE ALMOST LUMPER, BY FINN

NOUN _____

VERB (PAST TENSE) _____

PART OF THE BODY _____

ADJECTIVE _____

PLURAL NOUN _____

VERB _____

ADJECTIVE _____

NOUN _____

PART OF THE BODY _____

VERB _____

ADVERB _____

EXCLAMATION _____

ADJECTIVE _____

ADJECTIVE _____

NUMBER _____

PLURAL NOUN _____

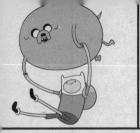

MAD LIBS
JAKE THE ALMOST LUMPER, BY FINN

This one time, Lumpy Space Princess accidentally bit Jake, and I was

all, "Holy _____ balls, bro! You're turning into a lumper!"
                NOUN

Jake _____ into a full-on lump. His _____
      VERB (PAST TENSE)   PART OF THE BODY

got way-puffy. His voice got super-_____. His mood
                                     ADJECTIVE

_____ were stank. And worst of all, he blew me off
  PLURAL NOUN

to _____ at the Lumpy Prom. If I didn't save him
      VERB

from a/an _____ lifetime of lump, no one would! I
            ADJECTIVE

scored the cure from some lumpers who were using it to keep their

_____ as smooth as a baby's _____. Then
     NOUN   PART OF THE BODY

I had them _____ me into a lumper with some bites
              VERB

so I could _____ float to the dance. There, Jake was
              ADVERB

all "_____! I don't want that lumping, _____
     EXCLAMATION   ADJECTIVE

cure!" My memory is a little _____ since my brain went
                              ADJECTIVE

_____ percent lump, but somehow we both got back to
   NUMBER

normal. We celebrated by shaking our _____ to groovy
                                        PLURAL NOUN

tunes. Epic win!

MAD LIBS® is fun to play with friends, but you can also play it by yourself! To begin with, DO NOT look at the story on the page below. Fill in the blanks on this page with the words called for. Then, using the words you have selected, fill in the blank spaces in the story.

Now you've created your own hilarious MAD LIBS® game!

WHY DON'T YOU LOVE ME, PRINCESSES EVERYWHERE?, BY ICE KING

ADJECTIVE _____

NOUN _____

PART OF THE BODY _____

EXCLAMATION _____

NOUN _____

ADJECTIVE _____

VERB ENDING IN "ING" _____

ADJECTIVE _____

NOUN _____

NOUN _____

VERB _____

PLURAL NOUN _____

NOUN _____

ADVERB _____

ADJECTIVE _____

NOUN _____

PLURAL NOUN _____

NOUN _____

MAD LIBS®
WHY DON'T YOU LOVE ME, PRINCESSES EVERYWHERE?, BY ICE KING

Dear _____ Princesses of Ooo,

ADJECTIVE

What does a single _____ like me need to do to get a bride

NOUN

around here? I've racked my _____ thinking up ways to

PART OF THE BODY

win your love, but you keep saying "_____! Get away from

EXCLAMATION

me, you psycho _____!" Is it my long, _____

NOUN — ADJECTIVE

beard that's scaring you? Because I tried _____ it off once

VERB ENDING IN "ING"

and you thought I was too nice! Is it my pointy, _____

ADJECTIVE

nose or my freezing, blue _____? You shouldn't judge a/an

NOUN

_____ by its cover, you know. Sure, I may _____

NOUN — VERB

you from your home and lock you up behind steel _____

PLURAL NOUN

on occasion, but it's only because I want to tie the _____

NOUN

and make you my _____ beloved wife! Is that so wrong?

ADVERB

How I wish to embrace you in a subzero, _____ hug!

ADJECTIVE

Princesses, can't you see I have a heart made of _____? I'd

NOUN

walk a million _____ to hypnotize you into saying "I do."

PLURAL NOUN

It's just the kind of _____ I am.

NOUN

From ADVENTURE TIME MAD LIBS® • ™ & © Cartoon Network. (s12).
Published by Price Stern Sloan, an imprint of Penguin Group (USA) Inc., 345 Hudson Street, New York, NY 10014.

MAD LIBS® is fun to play with friends, but you can also play it by yourself! To begin with, DO NOT look at the story on the page below. Fill in the blanks on this page with the words called for. Then, using the words you have selected, fill in the blank spaces in the story.

Now you've created your own hilarious MAD LIBS® game!

MY A+ APPLE PIE RECIPE, BY TREE TRUNKS

ADJECTIVE _____

NOUN _____

VERB _____

NOUN _____

ADJECTIVE _____

NUMBER _____

PLURAL NOUN _____

NOUN _____

COLOR _____

NOUN _____

NOUN _____

NUMBER _____

NOUN _____

ADJECTIVE _____

VERB ENDING IN "ING" _____

NOUN _____

PART OF THE BODY _____

COLOR _____

MAD LIBS®
MY A+ APPLE PIE RECIPE, BY TREE TRUNKS

Hi, y'all! Make a tasty, _____-fashioned apple pie
                        ADJECTIVE

with my step-by-_____ recipe! First, go outside and
                 NOUN

_____ the freshest apples right from the branch. I use my
  VERB

long _____ to reach up high! There should be no rotten or
     NOUN

_____ spots on your apples. Each one must be _____
ADJECTIVE   NUMBER

percent perfect! No ifs, ands, or _____ about it. Use a
                                  PLURAL NOUN

sharp _____ to carefully cut each apple into slices. Add 1
      NOUN

cup of _____ sugar, ¼ cup flour, and a tea-_____
       COLOR   NOUN

of cinnamon. Grab a wooden _____ and mix it all up!
                           NOUN

For the crust, combine _____ cups of flour, a pinch of
                       NUMBER

_____, 1 cup of butter, and ½ cup of _____
   NOUN   ADJECTIVE

water. Use a/an _____ pin to press the dough flat. Place
                VERB ENDING IN "ING"

the dough into a greased _____, then add the apples. Pop
                         NOUN

your pie in a warm oven and keep a close _____ on it.
                                         PART OF THE BODY

When the crust turns light _____, it's done!
                           COLOR

From ADVENTURE TIME MAD LIBS® • ™ & © Cartoon Network. (s12).
Published by Price Stern Sloan, an imprint of Penguin Group (USA) Inc., 345 Hudson Street, New York, NY 10014.

MAD LIBS® is fun to play with friends, but you can also play it by yourself! To begin with, DO NOT look at the story on the page below. Fill in the blanks on this page with the words called for. Then, using the words you have selected, fill in the blank spaces in the story.

Now you've created your own hilarious MAD LIBS® game!

HOW TO HANDLE A CANDY ZOMBIE ATTACK, BY PRINCESS BUBBLEGUM

ADJECTIVE _____

NOUN _____

VERB ENDING IN "ING" _____

ADJECTIVE _____

PLURAL NOUN _____

TYPE OF LIQUID _____

PLURAL NOUN _____

PLURAL NOUN _____

ADJECTIVE _____

VERB _____

PLURAL NOUN _____

NOUN _____

Uh-oh! Did your plan to revive _____ Candy
                                        ADJECTIVE

People result in zombification due to a malfunctioning decorpsinator

serum? Go back to the drawing _____ and correct the
                                        NOUN

serum formula immediately! Remember: Candy Zombies go on

a/an _____ frenzy when they're near sugar. Round up
        VERB ENDING IN "ING"

a group of tried-and-_____ non-sugary friends to keep
                            ADJECTIVE

the zombies from attacking innocent _____. Spraying
                                            PLURAL NOUN

a zombie with something sour, like pickle _____, will
                                                TYPE OF LIQUID

temporarily stop them in their _____. Most likely, the
                                    PLURAL NOUN

zombies are after one thing: Candy People! Candy People tend to

explode into bits and _____ when frightened, so keep
                            PLURAL NOUN

the zombies a secret! Try this: Tie a/an _____-fold around
                                            ADJECTIVE

their eyes. Shout "Piñata time!" and give each Candy Person a stick

to _____ in the air. Soon the zombies will be dropping like
        VERB

_____. And the best part? You can turn them back into healthy
PLURAL NOUN

_____ People once you've fixed the serum! Mathematical!
    NOUN

From ADVENTURE TIME MAD LIBS® • ™ & © Cartoon Network. (s12).
Published by Price Stern Sloan, an imprint of Penguin Group (USA) Inc., 345 Hudson Street, New York, NY 10014.

MAD LIBS® is fun to play with friends, but you can also play it by yourself! To begin with, DO NOT look at the story on the page below. Fill in the blanks on this page with the words called for. Then, using the words you have selected, fill in the blank spaces in the story.

Now you've created your own hilarious MAD LIBS® game!

SONG ABOUT OOO

VERB _____

ADJECTIVE _____

PART OF THE BODY (PLURAL) _____

NOUN _____

PLURAL NOUN _____

COLOR _____

ADJECTIVE _____

VERB ENDING IN "ING" _____

ADJECTIVE _____

NOUN _____

ANIMAL _____

EXCLAMATION _____

PART OF THE BODY _____

VERB ENDING IN "ING" _____

PLURAL NOUN _____

ADJECTIVE _____

NOUN _____

PART OF THE BODY _____

MAD LIBS®

SONG ABOUT OOO

Help Marceline _____ the lyrics to her catchy,
VERB

_____ song about her special spots in Ooo!
ADJECTIVE

I'm way old, like over a thousand, and my _____
PART OF THE BODY (PLURAL)

have seen so much stuff. No _____ about it, travelin's my
NOUN

habit, 'cause I can never get enough. I'm all aaah in Ooo! Like head

over _____ for Ooo! Suckin' out the _____
PLURAL NOUN   COLOR

from Strawberry Patch is the most _____ treat around.
ADJECTIVE

Love to thrash with my axe-bass. Tell me you're so _____
VERB ENDING IN "ING"

the sound. Ooo, my house is cozy, it's inside a deep, _____
ADJECTIVE

cave! Aaah, it's got a recording _____ plus my zombie pet
NOUN

_____, who's my fave. I'm all _____ in Ooo!
ANIMAL   EXCLAMATION

Like, _____ over heels for Ooo! Hula-_____
PART OF THE BODY   VERB ENDING IN "ING"

in the Fire Kingdom with hot _____ at my feet. Hangin' in
PLURAL NOUN

_____ Forest with the ghosties is sweet. Grasslands got my
ADJECTIVE

old pad, the _____ Fort. There's Finn and Jake who make
NOUN

my _____ totally snort. I'm way aaah for Ooo, yeahweeeooo!
PART OF THE BODY

From ADVENTURE TIME MAD LIBS® • ™ & © Cartoon Network. (s12).
Published by Price Stern Sloan, an imprint of Penguin Group (USA) Inc., 345 Hudson Street, New York, NY 10014.

MAD LIBS® is fun to play with friends, but you can also play it by yourself! To begin with, DO NOT look at the story on the page below. Fill in the blanks on this page with the words called for. Then, using the words you have selected, fill in the blank spaces in the story.

Now you've created your own hilarious MAD LIBS® game!

WHY I BECAME A MONSTER, BY LUMPY SPACE PRINCESS

NOUN _____

PLURAL NOUN _____

VERB ENDING IN "ING" _____

VERB _____

A PLACE _____

PLURAL NOUN _____

VERB _____

NOUN _____

PART OF THE BODY _____

PLURAL NOUN _____

NOUN _____

VERB _____

ADJECTIVE _____

NOUN _____

MAD LIBS®
WHY I BECAME A MONSTER, BY LUMPY SPACE PRINCESS

Did I ever tell you about the time I became a/an _____-eating

NOUN

monster? It all started when my lumping _____ and I got

PLURAL NOUN

into a major _____ match. I was all "_____

VERB ENDING IN "ING"   VERB

off!" and ran away. Drama bomb! In (the) _____, some

A PLACE

wolves took me under their _____ . . . until they totally

PLURAL NOUN

tried to _____ me into shreds! Whatever, wolves. You

VERB

never deserved my _____-ship! Finally I got away from

NOUN

those _____-stabbing wolves and ended up in a field

PART OF THE BODY

of fresh _____. The people there were all "Monster!"

PLURAL NOUN

So I pretended I was one and ate everything but the kitchen

_____. Actually, I ate that, too. I was starving, okay? But

NOUN

being a monster was no _____ in the park. I was lonely

VERB

and _____. Everyone was so mad at me for stealing their

ADJECTIVE

food. So when my parents sent Jake and Finn to bring me home, I

gave the people some of the _____-wiches my parents

NOUN

packed with Finn. I'm so lumping nice sometimes, right?

From ADVENTURE TIME MAD LIBS® • ™ & © Cartoon Network. (s12).
Published by Price Stern Sloan, an imprint of Penguin Group (USA) Inc., 345 Hudson Street, New York, NY 10014.

MAD LIBS® is fun to play with friends, but you can also play it by yourself! To begin with, DO NOT look at the story on the page below. Fill in the blanks on this page with the words called for. Then, using the words you have selected, fill in the blank spaces in the story.

Now you've created your own hilarious MAD LIBS® game!

WHAT'S AWESOME ABOUT LADY RAINICORN, BY JAKE

NOUN _____

NOUN _____

VERB ENDING IN "ING" _____

ADJECTIVE _____

VERB _____

PART OF THE BODY _____

PLURAL NOUN _____

NOUN _____

NOUN _____

ADJECTIVE _____

ADJECTIVE _____

PLURAL NOUN _____

NOUN _____

NUMBER _____

ADJECTIVE _____

NOUN _____

ADJECTIVE _____

Oh man. My _____-friend, Lady Rainicorn, is the coolest

NOUN

girl I've ever met! She's a total babe and a smart _____,

NOUN

too. We love _____ viola duets together. It's kinda our

VERB ENDING IN "ING"

thing. Her voice is so soft and _____, I could _____ to

ADJECTIVE   VERB

it forever, y'know? I'd bend over _____-ward for Lady.

PART OF THE BODY

Cuz I'm stretchy and stuff. She helps _____ in trouble,

PLURAL NOUN

too. Once Finn was being attacked by some meanie Lake Knights,

and she totally dove into the _____ and saved him! Did I

NOUN

mention how pretty she is? She's got _____-bow stripes

NOUN

on her body and a flowy, _____ mane. She smells like

ADJECTIVE

_____ roses and straw. Plus, she flies, dude! And she

ADJECTIVE

can go through _____ like a ghost!! And she can change

PLURAL NOUN

any color with her magical _____!!! Yep, my lady is

NOUN

_____ of a kind. I'm her _____ potato and

NUMBER   ADJECTIVE

she's my honey _____. We're mega-_____-

NOUN   ADJECTIVE

hearts like that.

MAD LIBS® is fun to play with friends, but you can also play it by yourself! To begin with, DO NOT look at the story on the page below. Fill in the blanks on this page with the words called for. Then, using the words you have selected, fill in the blank spaces in the story.

Now you've created your own hilarious MAD LIBS® game!

BMO'S PRIMO FEATURES, BY BMO

VERB ENDING IN "ING" _____

PLURAL NOUN _____

ADJECTIVE _____

ADJECTIVE _____

NOUN _____

NOUN _____

NOUN _____

PLURAL NOUN _____

PART OF THE BODY (PLURAL) _____

PLURAL NOUN _____

NOUN _____

PLURAL NOUN _____

ADJECTIVE _____

PLURAL NOUN _____

ADJECTIVE _____

MAD☺LIBS®

BMO'S PRIMO FEATURES, BY BMO

Hi. I am BMO. I live with Jake and Finn. They spend hours

_____ video games on me. There are two
　　VERB ENDING IN "ING"

_____ on my front for joysticks to plug into. Once, Jake
　　PLURAL NOUN

and Finn made me press my _____ button when they
　　　　　　　　　　　　　　　　ADJECTIVE

tickled me. This sent them into a very _____ place—my
　　　　　　　　　　　　　　　　　　ADJECTIVE

main-brain-_____-frame! They went inside the video
　　　　　　　NOUN

_____, but *whew!* they got out alive. I am also alarm
　　NOUN

_____ for when it is time for Finn to take bath. I love to
　　NOUN

take pictures, too. The finished _____ shoot out of my
　　　　　　　　　　　　　　　　　PLURAL NOUN

_____. It is silly, but that is how I work! I can play
PART OF THE BODY (PLURAL)

VHS _____. We watched a whole lot of ones that the
　　　PLURAL NOUN

_____ King made. He gives me heebie-_____.
　　NOUN　　　　　　　　　　　　　　　　　　　　　　PLURAL NOUN

If you need power source, I have extra _____ outlet! One
　　　　　　　　　　　　　　　　　　　ADJECTIVE

thing I am not is a place for Jake to rest his _____! I get
　　　　　　　　　　　　　　　　　　　　　　PLURAL NOUN

_____ face when that happens. But mostly I am happy
　　ADJECTIVE

BMO and always have smile for you!

From ADVENTURE TIME MAD LIBS® • ™ & © Cartoon Network. (s12).
Published by Price Stern Sloan, an imprint of Penguin Group (USA) Inc., 345 Hudson Street, New York, NY 10014.

MAD LIBS® is fun to play with friends, but you can also play it by yourself! To begin with, DO NOT look at the story on the page below. Fill in the blanks on this page with the words called for. Then, using the words you have selected, fill in the blank spaces in the story.

Now you've created your own hilarious MAD LIBS® game!

HOW TO WIN FRIENDS WITH LOTS OF TRYING AND A LITTLE MAGIC, BY ICE KING

VERB _____

NOUN _____

NOUN _____

NOUN _____

NOUN _____

ADJECTIVE _____

PLURAL NOUN _____

ADJECTIVE _____

NOUN _____

NOUN _____

NUMBER _____

VERB ENDING IN "ING" _____

NOUN _____

MAD LIBS®
HOW TO WIN FRIENDS
WITH LOTS OF TRYING AND
A LITTLE MAGIC, BY ICE KING

Wish you met someone who doesn't _____ in the other
VERB

direction when you arrive? Follow my solid-as-_____
NOUN

guidelines and watch your popularity _____-rocket!
NOUN

Rule #1: Every living _____ is a potential pal. If your
NOUN

only confidant is the reflection in your _____, try
NOUN

chatting up that _____ plant in the corner and see what
ADJECTIVE

happens! *Rule #2:* Don't be afraid to spy on _____ you'd
PLURAL NOUN

like to know better. You'll learn a lot about your _____
ADJECTIVE

friend that way, and they'll be impressed you know what they ate

for _____-fast! *Rule #3:* It's okay to ring someone's
NOUN

door-_____ more than _____ times in a
NOUN   NUMBER

row even if you're not "invited." *Rule #4:* Nothing is wrong with

_____ your future friends with a freezing potion to
VERB ENDING IN "ING"

make 'em stick around! *Rule #5:* Beg somebody, anybody, to throw

you a/an _____-day party. Don't stop until they do. It'll be
NOUN

the best party ever!

From ADVENTURE TIME MAD LIBS® • ™ & © Cartoon Network. (s12).
Published by Price Stern Sloan, an imprint of Penguin Group (USA) Inc., 345 Hudson Street, New York, NY 10014.

MAD LIBS® is fun to play with friends, but you can also play it by yourself! To begin with, DO NOT look at the story on the page below. Fill in the blanks on this page with the words called for. Then, using the words you have selected, fill in the blank spaces in the story.

Now you've created your own hilarious MAD LIBS® game!

WELCOME TO CANDY KINGDOM!

PLURAL NOUN _____

NOUN _____

VERB _____

NOUN _____

ADJECTIVE _____

PLURAL NOUN _____

NOUN _____

ADJECTIVE _____

NOUN _____

NOUN _____

ADJECTIVE _____

NOUN _____

ANIMAL _____

VERB ENDING IN "ING" _____

NOUN _____

ADJECTIVE _____

VERB ENDING IN "ING" _____

NOUN _____

MAD LIBS®
WELCOME TO CANDY KINGDOM!

Come meet the most sugary _____ in all of Ooo! Princess
                            PLURAL NOUN

Bubble-_____ is the leader of the Candy People. She is
           NOUN

kind and smart, but don't _____ her path! PB fights tooth
                           VERB

and _____ to shield her citizens from danger. The Banana
      NOUN

Guards make sure no _____ guys get into the castle.
                      ADJECTIVE

They have popsicle _____ for feet. Peppermint Butler is
                    PLURAL NOUN

PB's personal _____. He has a/an _____ IQ and a
               NOUN   ADJECTIVE

mysterious past. Starchy is a chocolate malt _____ and works
                                               NOUN

in the cemetery as a/an _____-digger. Cinnamon Bun is
                          NOUN

a bit _____-baked and isn't the smartest _____
       ADJECTIVE   NOUN

in the shed. Science is a candy corn lab _____. He's
                                           ANIMAL

really good at _____ formulas. Mr. Cupcake
                VERB ENDING IN "ING"

is a/an _____-builder and likes to show off his large,
          NOUN

_____ muscles. _____ under the weather?
  ADJECTIVE   VERB ENDING IN "ING"

Nurse _____-cake, Dr. Ice Cream, and Dr. Princess keep
       NOUN

everyone in tip-top shape!

From ADVENTURE TIME MAD LIBS® • ™ & © Cartoon Network. (s12).
Published by Price Stern Sloan, an imprint of Penguin Group (USA) Inc., 345 Hudson Street, New York, NY 10014.

MAD LIBS® is fun to play with friends, but you can also play it by yourself! To begin with, DO NOT look at the story on the page below. Fill in the blanks on this page with the words called for. Then, using the words you have selected, fill in the blank spaces in the story.

Now you've created your own hilarious MAD LIBS® game!

JAKE'S SWEETEST, STRETCHIEST MOVES

NOUN _____

ADJECTIVE _____

VERB ENDING IN "ING" _____

NOUN _____

NOUN _____

NUMBER _____

VERB _____

NOUN _____

VERB _____

NOUN _____

EXCLAMATION _____

ADVERB _____

NOUN _____

VERB _____

Jake's not your average, run-of-the-_____ bulldog. Nope, he's
                                              NOUN

got _____ Powers! He was probably born with them, but
        ADJECTIVE

Jake thinks he got them from _____ in a magic mud
                                    VERB ENDING IN "ING"

puddle. The powers let Jake shape-shift into all sorts of things. If he

needs to hide, he can shrink himself down to fit inside Finn's front

shirt _____. Or if Finn is in a sticky _____,
          NOUN   NOUN

Jake can inflate over _____ times his regular size and
                            NUMBER

help him out. Sometimes Jake's powers don't _____
                                                    VERB

that well. To unlock a door, Jake can turn his hand into the shape

of a/an _____ . . . but it usually doesn't fit. Once,
              NOUN

Jake and Finn were stuck in BMO's video game and needed to

_____ a pit. Jake was able to stretch his _____
    VERB   NOUN

to safety. _____, right? Then there was the time Jake
              EXCLAMATION

stretched himself too _____ while in a maze and almost
                            ADVERB

kicked the _____. Mostly, he uses his powers to make Finn
                NOUN

_____ really hard!
    VERB

From ADVENTURE TIME MAD LIBS® • ™ & © Cartoon Network. (s12).
Published by Price Stern Sloan, an imprint of Penguin Group (USA) Inc., 345 Hudson Street, New York, NY 10014.

MAD LIBS® is fun to play with friends, but you can also play it by yourself! To begin with, DO NOT look at the story on the page below. Fill in the blanks on this page with the words called for. Then, using the words you have selected, fill in the blank spaces in the story.

Now you've created your own hilarious MAD LIBS® game!

THE DAY WE ROCKED SO FLIPPIN' HARD, BY FINN

COLOR _____

PLURAL NOUN _____

NOUN _____

ADJECTIVE _____

ADJECTIVE _____

VERB _____

ADJECTIVE _____

VERB _____

VERB ENDING IN "ING" _____

PLURAL NOUN _____

PART OF THE BODY _____

ADJECTIVE _____

PLURAL NOUN _____

MAD LIBS®
THE DAY WE ROCKED SO FLIPPIN' HARD, BY FINN

Ever hear about the time me and my buds formed a/an

_____-hot band? It all started when a Door Lord
COLOR

stole our precious _____. He took BMO's controller,
PLURAL NOUN

Jake's baby _____, and, um, uh . . . a wad of Princess
NOUN

Bubblegum's _____ hair that I sometimes cuddle with.
ADJECTIVE

We stayed _____ on his trail. He lived behind a sealed
ADJECTIVE

door that said *"This door shall _____ to no command,*
VERB

save for a song from a/an _____ band." We had to
ADJECTIVE

_____ music together to bust open that door! First,
VERB

everyone was _____ like cats and _____. Then
VERB ENDING IN "ING"   PLURAL NOUN

we realized that not just any song would work—it had to be one

that came from the _____. So I started crooning about
PART OF THE BODY

how everyone there was my best friend in the whole, _____
ADJECTIVE

world. My pals joined in and the door opened! I think we all learned

that the real treasure is being good _____ together. But I'm
PLURAL NOUN

glad I got PB's hair back.

MAD LIBS® is fun to play with friends, but you can also play it by yourself! To begin with, DO NOT look at the story on the page below. Fill in the blanks on this page with the words called for. Then, using the words you have selected, fill in the blank spaces in the story.

Now you've created your own hilarious MAD LIBS® game!

HOW TO PICK THE BEST HENCHMAN, BY MARCELINE

NOUN _____

ADJECTIVE _____

NOUN _____

NOUN _____

NUMBER _____

VERB _____

PLURAL NOUN _____

VERB _____

ADJECTIVE _____

PLURAL NOUN _____

PART OF THE BODY _____

NOUN _____

ADJECTIVE _____

NOUN _____

ADJECTIVE _____

PART OF THE BODY _____

NOUN _____

MAD LIBS®
HOW TO PICK THE BEST HENCHMAN, BY MARCELINE

Need a side-_____ to do all your _____
                    NOUN   ADJECTIVE

work? Check out my tips on how to choose the right guy or

_____ for the job.
       NOUN

1. Find someone who will go the extra _____ for you.
                                              NOUN

   It's good if they think you're _____ percent evil and
                                         NUMBER

   you _____ the living day-_____ out of them.
         VERB   PLURAL NOUN

2. If your henchman refuses to follow orders, _____ the
                                                    VERB

   command in a stern, _____ tone. It helps them listen better.
                        ADJECTIVE

3. The ideal henchman doesn't ask too many _____ or
                                              PLURAL NOUN

   really use their _____ to think at all.
                    PART OF THE BODY

Finn was my best _____-man at first, but it didn't
                        NOUN

last because he got real _____ to my tricks! Having a
                            ADJECTIVE

henchman who is as sharp as a/an _____ just doesn't
                                      NOUN

last in the _____ run. Cuz once they realize that you're
              ADJECTIVE

just pulling their _____ with the whole "I'm a/an
                    PART OF THE BODY

_____-sucking vampire" thing, your game is so up.
       NOUN

From ADVENTURE TIME MAD LIBS® • ™ & © Cartoon Network. (s12).
Published by Price Stern Sloan, an imprint of Penguin Group (USA) Inc., 345 Hudson Street, New York, NY 10014.

MAD LIBS® is fun to play with friends, but you can also play it by yourself! To begin with, DO NOT look at the story on the page below. Fill in the blanks on this page with the words called for. Then, using the words you have selected, fill in the blank spaces in the story.

Now you've created your own hilarious MAD LIBS® game!

THE PERFECT PRANK, BY PRINCESS BUBBLEGUM

NUMBER _____

PART OF THE BODY _____

NOUN _____

ADJECTIVE _____

NOUN _____

ADJECTIVE _____

PLURAL NOUN _____

ADJECTIVE _____

VERB (PAST TENSE) _____

ADJECTIVE _____

NOUN _____

PLURAL NOUN _____

NUMBER _____

PLURAL NOUN _____

PART OF THE BODY _____

NOUN _____

THE PERFECT PRANK, BY PRINCESS BUBBLEGUM

When I aged myself down to _____ years old, things
                              NUMBER

got a little out of _____ in Candy Kingdom. The Earl of
                    PART OF THE BODY

Lemongrab rode in on his royal _____ and said I was too
                                NOUN

_____ to rule! According to the rule _____,
ADJECTIVE   NOUN

he was right. But the earl was a mean, _____ tyrant.
                                        ADJECTIVE

I had to get him to pack up his _____ and leave for
                                PLURAL NOUN

good. Finn and I decided to play _____ pranks on him!
                                 ADJECTIVE

First, we set up a machine where a boot _____ a marble
                                        VERB (PAST TENSE)

which set off a/an _____ reaction of motion. The final
                   ADJECTIVE

result was a note that sprang up for the earl to read. It said "You

smell like hot _____ buns." Then, we dressed up like
               NOUN

spooky _____ and tried to scare him out of town. Well,
       PLURAL NOUN

that didn't work! We were back to square _____. But we
                                         NUMBER

had one more prank up our _____. We poured spicy
                          PLURAL NOUN

serum right into his _____. You could say he got a/an
                     PART OF THE BODY

_____ of his own medicine!
NOUN

MAD LIBS® is fun to play with friends, but you can also play it by yourself! To begin with, DO NOT look at the story on the page below. Fill in the blanks on this page with the words called for. Then, using the words you have selected, fill in the blank spaces in the story.

Now you've created your own hilarious MAD LIBS® game!

ME VS. THE OCEAN, BY FINN

VERB (PAST TENSE) _____

PART OF THE BODY (PLURAL) _____

VERB _____

ADJECTIVE _____

NOUN _____

PLURAL NOUN _____

ADJECTIVE _____

EXCLAMATION _____

NOUN _____

VERB (PAST TENSE) _____

PART OF THE BODY _____

PART OF THE BODY _____

NOUN _____

ADJECTIVE _____

VERB ENDING IN "ING"_____

MAD LIBS®
ME VS. THE OCEAN, BY FINN

I didn't even know the ocean totally _____ me out until I
<u>VERB (PAST TENSE)</u>

tried to go in! When the waves came close, my _____
<u>PART OF THE BODY (PLURAL)</u>

trembled like crazy. So not math. How could I be a real hero if I

didn't _____ my fear? That's why I asked Jake for help.
<u>VERB</u>

He took me for an _____ submarine ride. We saw
<u>ADJECTIVE</u>

an abandoned old _____ and sea-_____. I
<u>NOUN</u>   <u>PLURAL NOUN</u>

was beginning to dig the ocean until Jake steered us into a deep,

_____ abyss! "_____!" I screamed. I
<u>ADJECTIVE</u>   <u>EXCLAMATION</u>

pulled the emergency _____ on my diving suit and
<u>NOUN</u>

_____ to the surface. All that commotion made Jake hit
<u>VERB (PAST TENSE)</u>

his _____ hard, knocking him out! I had to save him, but
<u>PART OF THE BODY</u>

my fear was huge. So I knocked myself on the _____
<u>PART OF THE BODY</u>

with a/an _____ and landed near Jake. Once I realized
<u>NOUN</u>

where I was, I panicked. Jake pulled his cord and soon we were back

on _____ land. Does being scared make me less than a
<u>ADJECTIVE</u>

hero? No _____ way!
<u>VERB ENDING IN "ING"</u>

From ADVENTURE TIME MAD LIBS® • ™ & © Cartoon Network. (s12).
Published by Price Stern Sloan, an imprint of Penguin Group (USA) Inc., 345 Hudson Street, New York, NY 10014.

MAD LIBS® is fun to play with friends, but you can also play it by yourself! To begin with, DO NOT look at the story on the page below. Fill in the blanks on this page with the words called for. Then, using the words you have selected, fill in the blank spaces in the story.

Now you've created your own hilarious MAD LIBS® game!

THE BLAME GAME, BY JAKE & FINN

COLOR _____

VERB (PAST TENSE) _____

PLURAL NOUN _____

PART OF THE BODY (PLURAL) _____

NOUN _____

VERB _____

ADJECTIVE _____

PLURAL NOUN _____

NOUN _____

ADJECTIVE _____

NOUN _____

VERB _____

MAD LIBS
THE BLAME GAME,
BY JAKE & FINN

Finn: Yo, Jake, remember that time one of our righteous spells turned Princess Bubblegum's skin _____ and her hair
<u>_____</u> out?
COLOR
VERB (PAST TENSE)

Jake: Oh yeah! And she blamed the Duke of _____ for it.
PLURAL NOUN

Man, she hated his _____.
PART OF THE BODY (PLURAL)

Finn: When she was all "I won't forgive the _____ who
NOUN

did this to me," I couldn't _____ up to the truth. We went
VERB

after the duke. Not my most _____ moment as a hero.
ADJECTIVE

Jake: S'ok. Even awesome _____ like us make mistakes.
PLURAL NOUN

Finn: We went to find the duke and he was sweeter than _____!
NOUN

Jake: Well, he did fess up to stealing all of PB's _____
ADJECTIVE

pudding supply.

Finn: And we fessed up to PB for making her look like an ugly

_____.
NOUN

Jake: And she didn't _____ it against us! But she still doesn't
VERB

like the duke. Whatevs!

From ADVENTURE TIME MAD LIBS® • ™ & © Cartoon Network. (s12).
Published by Price Stern Sloan, an imprint of Penguin Group (USA) Inc., 345 Hudson Street, New York, NY 10014.

MAD LIBS® is fun to play with friends, but you can also play it by yourself! To begin with, DO NOT look at the story on the page below. Fill in the blanks on this page with the words called for. Then, using the words you have selected, fill in the blank spaces in the story.

Now you've created your own hilarious MAD LIBS® game!

POEM FOR PRINCESS BUBBLEGUM, BY FINN

NOUN _____

ADJECTIVE _____

VERB _____

ADJECTIVE _____

PLURAL NOUN _____

VERB _____

NOUN _____

PART OF THE BODY (PLURAL) _____

VERB _____

PLURAL NOUN _____

ADJECTIVE _____

ADJECTIVE _____

NOUN _____

ADJECTIVE _____

MAD LIBS®
POEM FOR PRINCESS BUBBLEGUM, BY FINN

Oh, PB, I miss the _____ we shared when you were
                              NOUN

thirteen. Your lips tasted so _____. Do you think we'll
                                    ADJECTIVE

ever repeat that scene? There's so much to like about you, I can't

even _____ that high. If I got on your _____
          VERB   ADJECTIVE

side, I think I'd just about die. Love that you love science. You're so

math. Plus you fight the bad _____ and all evil wrath.
                                    PLURAL NOUN

Whenever we _____ time together, my heart goes *tick-*
                    VERB

tock-tick. By now you gotta know that I think you're so algebraic.

Do you think it's weird that I have a/an _____ of your
                                                  NOUN

hair? Or that when I look into your _____ all I can
                                        PART OF THE BODY (PLURAL)

do is _____ and stare? You can brush me off as a crush,
          VERB

but my _____ won't disappear. No one can match your
            PLURAL NOUN

_____ smile. Am I making myself clear? Basically you're
    ADJECTIVE

the most _____ girl I've ever known. And if you don't like
              ADJECTIVE

me more than a/an _____, I guess I'll just be alone. This
                        NOUN

poem you'll never see, it's way too _____ to share. Just
                                          ADJECTIVE

know, that I'll always supercare.

MAD LIBS® is fun to play with friends, but you can also play it by yourself! To begin with, DO NOT look at the story on the page below. Fill in the blanks on this page with the words called for. Then, using the words you have selected, fill in the blank spaces in the story.

Now you've created your own hilarious MAD LIBS® game!

THAT LUMPING BRAD!, BY LUMPY SPACE PRINCESS

NOUN _____

VERB ENDING IN "ING" _____

ADJECTIVE _____

NOUN _____

ADJECTIVE _____

NOUN _____

FIRST NAME (FEMALE) _____

VERB _____

NOUN _____

PART OF THE BODY (PLURAL) _____

ADJECTIVE _____

NOUN _____

NOUN _____

ADJECTIVE _____

PART OF THE BODY (PLURAL) _____

NOUN _____

MAD LIBS®

THAT LUMPING BRAD!, BY LUMPY SPACE PRINCESS

What the _____, you guys! I can't stop _____
NOUN   VERB ENDING IN "ING"

about my stupid, _____ ex-boyfriend, Brad. He's like
ADJECTIVE

my best dream and my worst _____-mare all rolled
NOUN

up into one smallish, _____ body. I'm telling you,
ADJECTIVE

we were a/an _____ made in space heaven! So why is
NOUN

he going out with my best friend, _____? I mean,
FIRST NAME (FEMALE)

I _____ her to death but she doesn't deserve him! Life
VERB

is so unfair! She's always teasing me about how she's Brad's girl-

_____. It makes me cry my _____
NOUN   PART OF THE BODY (PLURAL)

out all the lumping time. And then my face gets all red and

_____. I can't take it! They're probably eating chili
ADJECTIVE

_____ fries like we used to do right now. Traitors! Can
NOUN

I tell you something? I broke up with Brad. But he broke my

_____ into a million teensy, _____ pieces! He
NOUN   ADJECTIVE

kissed me on the _____, and I just wasn't ready.
PART OF THE BODY (PLURAL)

Oh my _____, you guys, I want him back so bad!!
NOUN

MAD LIBS® is fun to play with friends, but you can also play it by yourself! To begin with, DO NOT look at the story on the page below. Fill in the blanks on this page with the words called for. Then, using the words you have selected, fill in the blank spaces in the story.

Now you've created your own hilarious MAD LIBS® game!

COME HANG IN THE TREE FORT!

ADJECTIVE _____

PLURAL NOUN _____

NOUN _____

ADJECTIVE _____

COLOR _____

NOUN _____

VERB ENDING IN "ING" _____

NOUN _____

VERB _____

NOUN _____

NOUN _____

ADJECTIVE _____

VERB _____

NOUN _____

ADJECTIVE _____

NOUN _____

VERB _____

COME HANG IN
THE TREE FORT!

Finn and Jake's Tree Fort is their home _____ home.
ADJECTIVE

The tree has lots of nooks and _____ to explore, so let's
PLURAL NOUN

take a peek! The entrance is at the base of the _____
NOUN

trunk. Once you're inside, there are all sorts of treasures, like piles of

_____ coins, old black-and-_____ TVs, and a
ADJECTIVE   COLOR

uni-_____. A ladder leads up to the _____
NOUN   VERB ENDING IN "ING"

room. That's where Finn and Jake have their weekly _____
NOUN

club, play with BMO, and just generally hang. In the kitchen, Jake

likes to _____ up culinary masterpieces. Climb another
VERB

_____ to get to the bedroom. Finn snuggles up in a sleeping
NOUN

_____ and Jake slumbers in a/an _____ dresser
NOUN   ADJECTIVE

drawer. Near the top of the tree, there's a/an _____-out
VERB

boat with a tele-_____ to check out what's happening in
NOUN

the distance. A few outdoor bridges provide _____ access to
ADJECTIVE

different floors. Of course, no fort would be complete without a roof

for _____-gazing and _____-butt dance parties!
NOUN   VERB

From ADVENTURE TIME MAD LIBS® • ™ & © Cartoon Network. (s12).
Published by Price Stern Sloan, an imprint of Penguin Group (USA) Inc., 345 Hudson Street, New York, NY 10014.

MAD LIBS® is fun to play with friends, but you can also play it by yourself! To begin with, DO NOT look at the story on the page below. Fill in the blanks on this page with the words called for. Then, using the words you have selected, fill in the blank spaces in the story.

Now you've created your own hilarious MAD LIBS® game!

HOW TO BE A HERO IN FIVE EASY STEPS

NOUN _____

VERB ENDING IN "ING" _____

VERB _____

NUMBER _____

ADJECTIVE _____

NOUN _____

NOUN _____

PLURAL NOUN _____

NOUN _____

ADJECTIVE _____

NOUN _____

NOUN _____

ADJECTIVE _____

VERB _____

NOUN _____

MAD LIBS®
HOW TO BE A HERO IN FIVE EASY STEPS

Go from a wrongteous zero to a happenin' _____ by
                                              NOUN

_____ a few righteous rules!
VERB ENDING IN "ING"

1. No matter what, heroes will always _____ evil wherever
                                            VERB

   it may be. Even if evil is living _____ thousand miles
                                          NUMBER

   away in a really inconvenient location like the middle of a/an

   _____ desert or beneath a deep, smelly _____.
      ADJECTIVE   NOUN

2. Heroes don't have to put on a brave _____ all the time.
                                             NOUN

   But they still save the day even when they're feeling like giant

   scaredy _____.
           PLURAL NOUN

3. A hero puts his _____ on the line to protect anyone
                         NOUN

   who needs help. Usually this includes little _____
                                                      ADJECTIVE

   ladies, a kidnapped _____, and your best friend.
                            NOUN

4. A hero makes someone feel like they're on top of the _____!
                                                              NOUN

5. It's okay for a hero to make a/an _____ mistake. Don't
                                          ADJECTIVE

   _____ yourself up if you mess up! Just get back on the
      VERB

   right _____ and soon you'll be all hero-y in no time!
            NOUN

Shmowzow!

Published by Price Stern Sloan, an imprint of Penguin Group (USA) Inc., 345 Hudson Street, New York, NY 10014.